Edition Schott

Morton Subotnick

b. 1933

The Other Piano

for Piano

für Klavier

ED 30024

ISMN M-800011-03-0

www.schott-music.com

Mainz · London · Madrid · New York · Paris · Prague · Tokyo · Toronto
© 2008 SCHOTT MUSIC CORPORATION · Printed in USA

Preface

About *The Other Piano*:

The Other Piano is scored for piano, with or without surround sound processing. If the piece is performed without processing, there are three continuous sections: *Lullaby* (1); *Alone* (2); *Rocking* (3). If it is performed with processing, there are four continuous sections: *Within* (0); *Lullaby* (1); *Alone* (2); *Rocking* (3). The title is a tribute to the memory of Morty Feldman. I was with him at the premiere of his work, *Piano*. He told me once that a friend called and congratulated him on marrying Joan La Barbara. He replied, "Thanks, but that was the other Morty." *The Other Piano* was written for Vicki Ray, who premiered it on May 1, 2007 at Zipper Hall in Los Angeles.

About processing the piano:

There is no processing score or computer patch—only instructions which give the general intention of what is expected for each section of the work. If possible, the processing should be immersive, with at least four speakers in the four corners of the space. The processed sound should always be below the level of the actual piano sound, as if it were a dream-like manifestation of the performance.

Suggestions:

In *Within*, I used a simulation of rotating speakers and granular delay with a varied delay timing. In addition, I used an octave shifter to make the delayed version of the piano sound even lower than it actually was. (This was used mostly in the repeated, semi-improvised section.) The surround movement was subtle, except in the loud improvised section. There, I used quick, circular pans of the space.

In *Lullaby*, I primarily used a bank of plug-ins (including Freeverb3) which allowed for varied reverb and the ability to freeze notes at will. In addition, I used other plug-ins for slight detuning of the piano.

In *Many*, I used granular delay, detuning with more active surround movement. At times, the movement was randomized.

In *Rocking*, I used a subtle version of the rotating speaker effect. This caused a kind of gentle throbbing, almost like the gentle rocking of a baby. The surround movement was a very slow back-and-forth across the space.

Morton Subotnick
2008

Contents

O
Within
[Remembering Morty]

Morton Subotnick

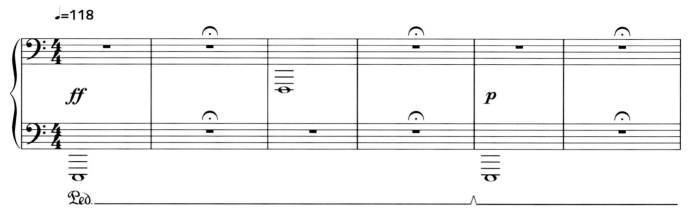

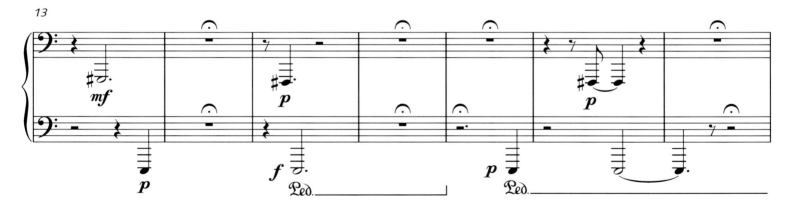

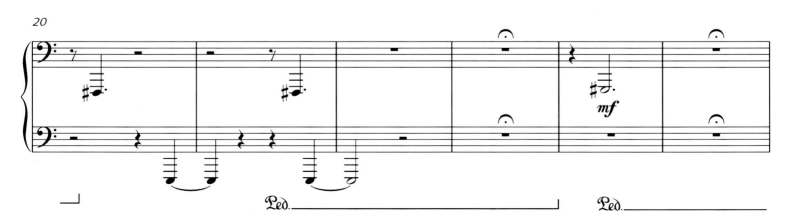

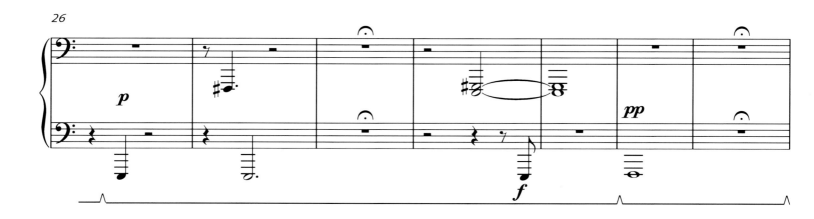

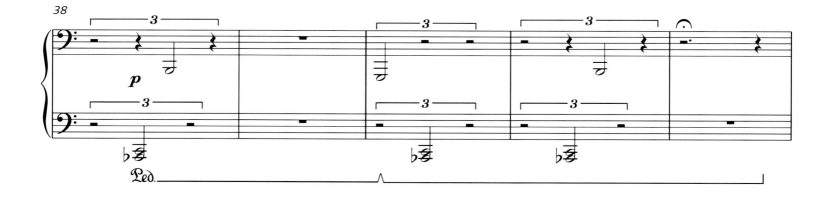

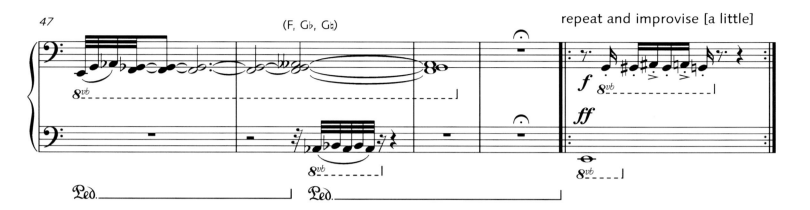

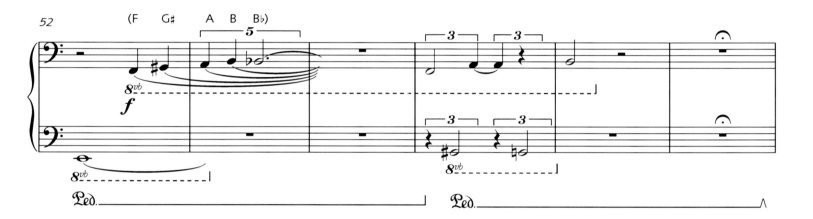

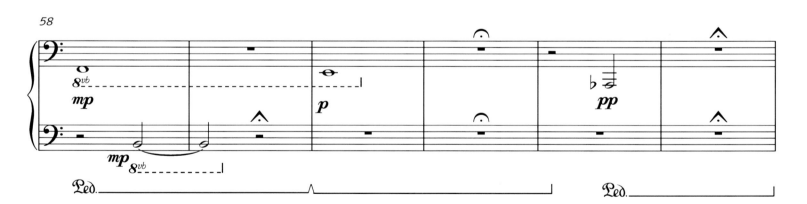

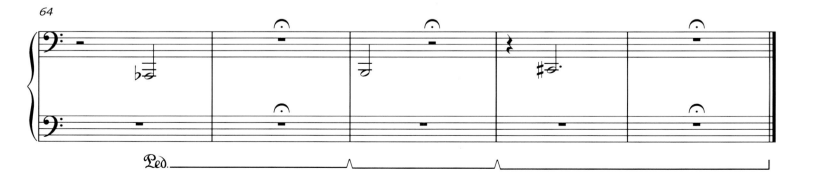

1
Lullaby

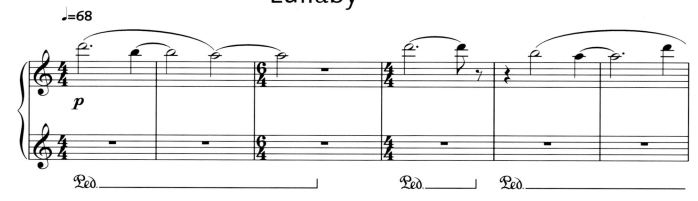

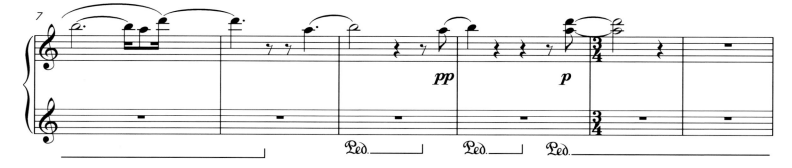

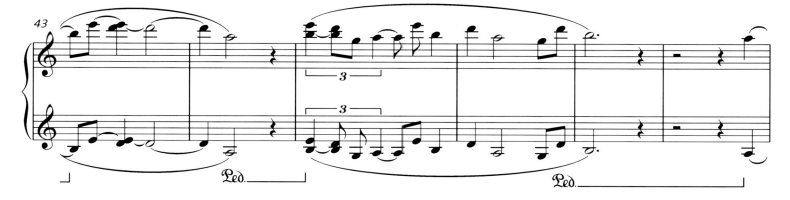

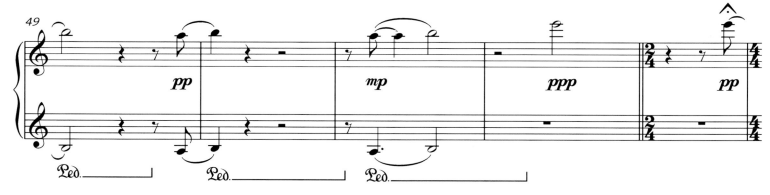

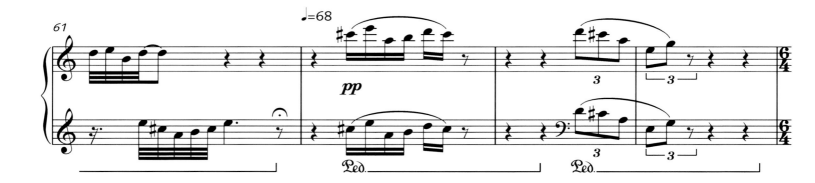

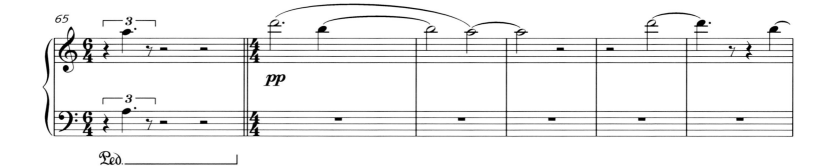

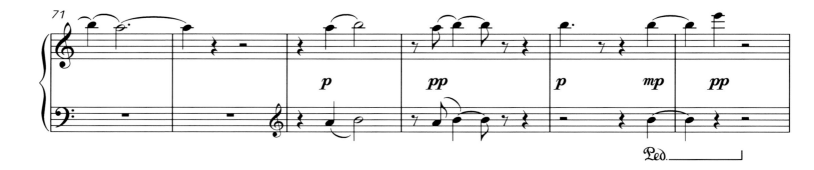

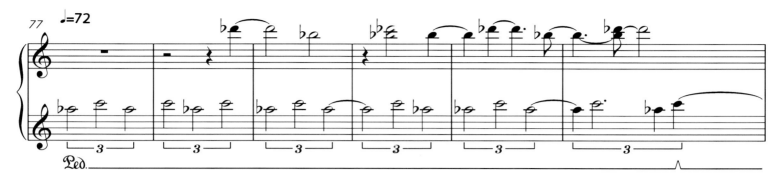

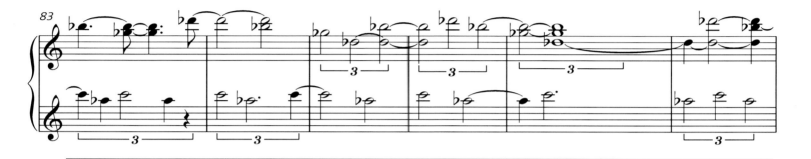

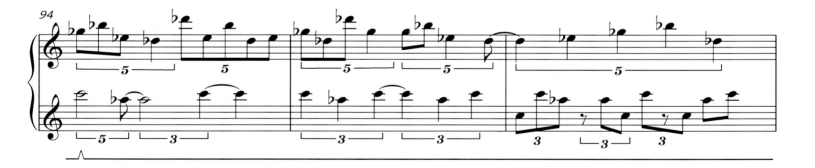

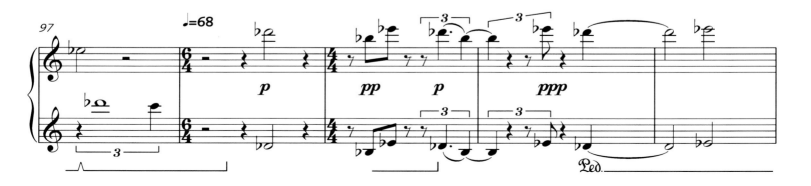

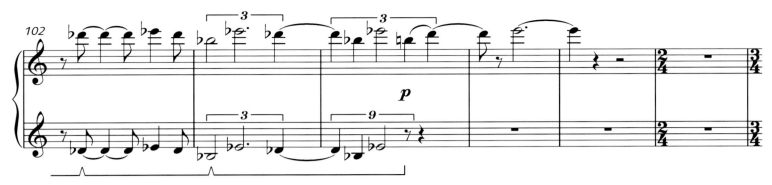

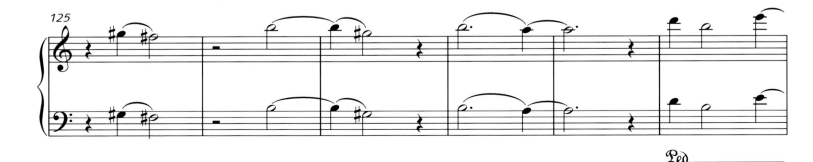

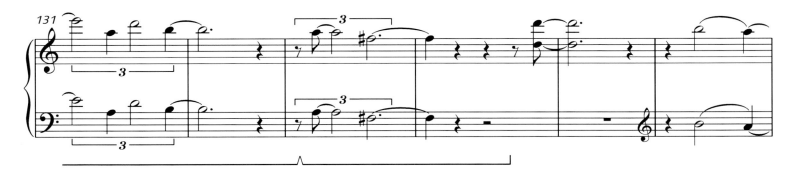

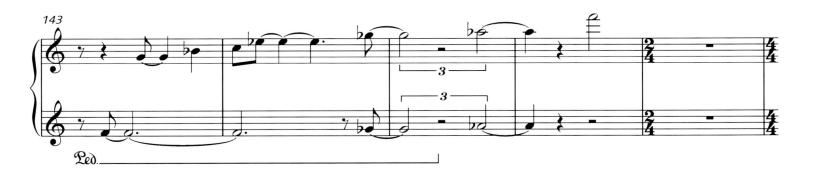

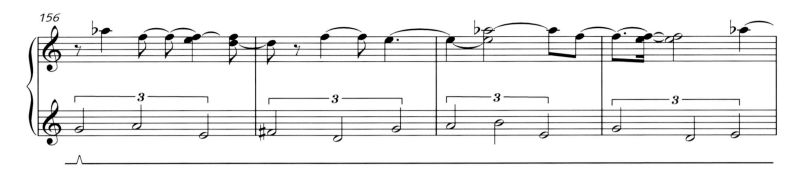

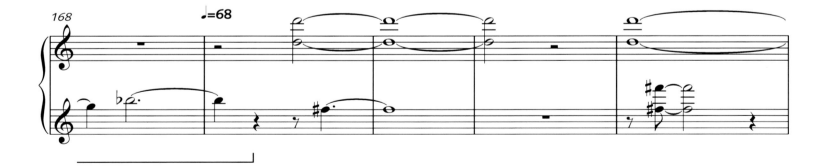

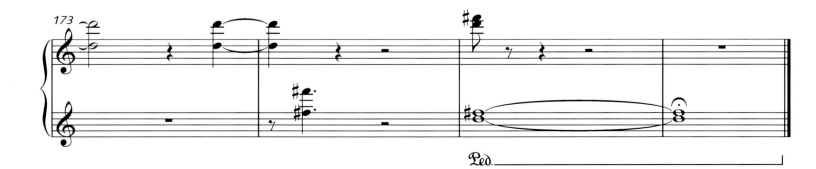

2
Many

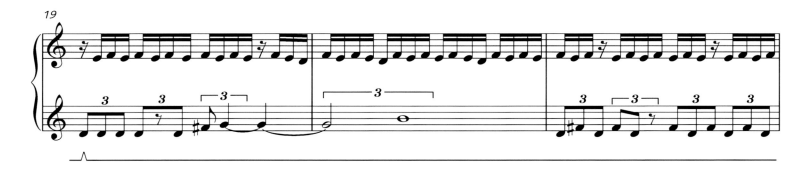

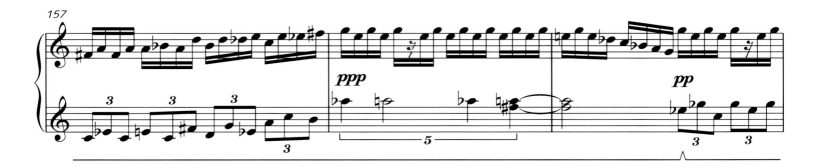

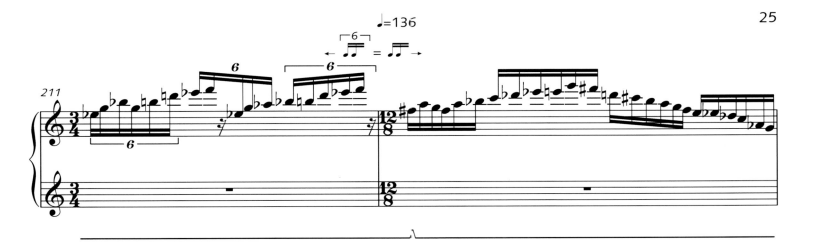

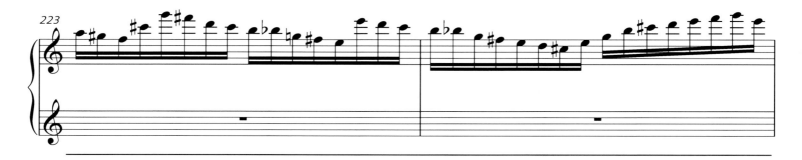

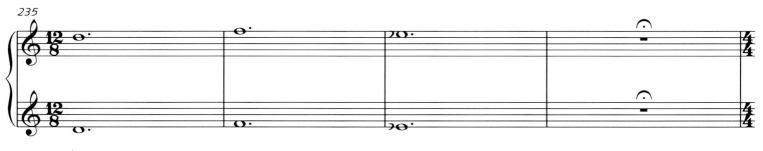

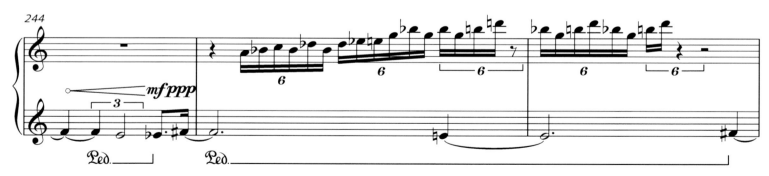

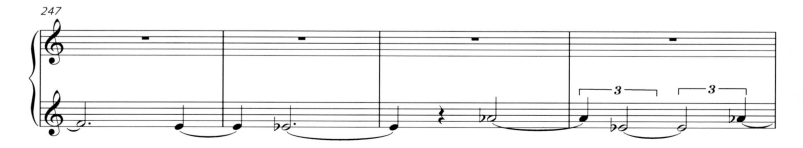

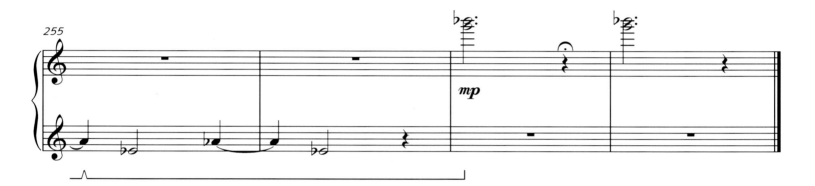

3
Rocking

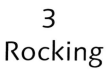

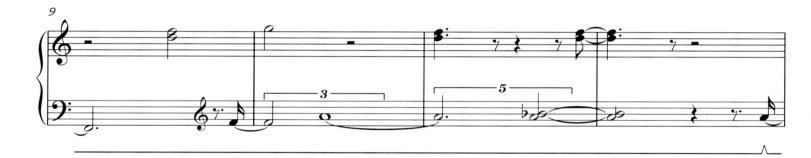

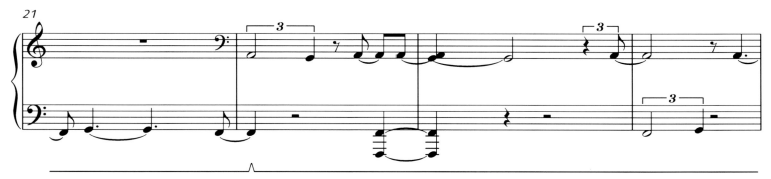

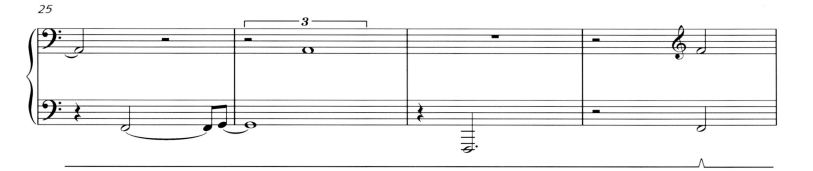

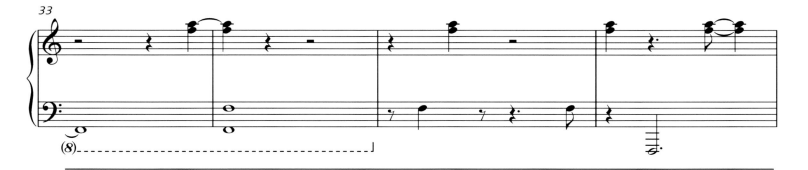

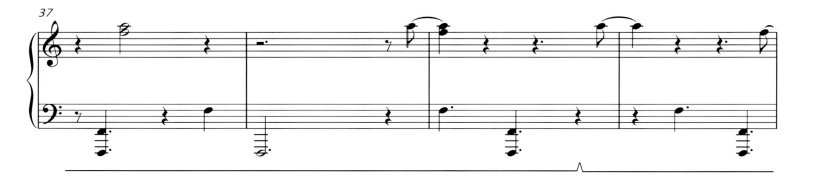

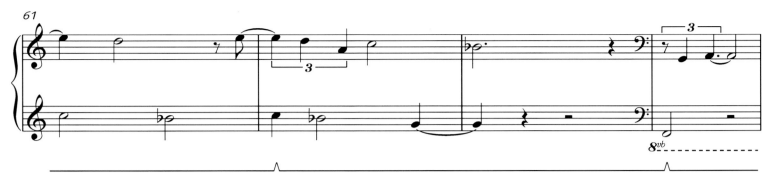

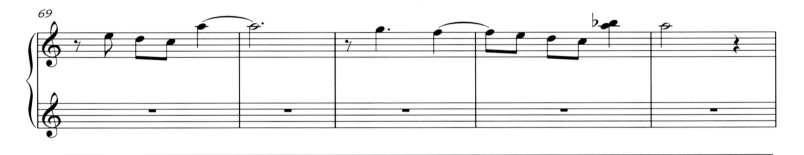

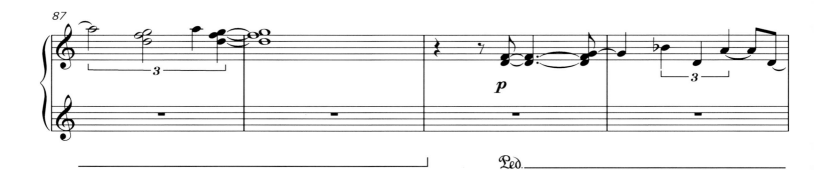

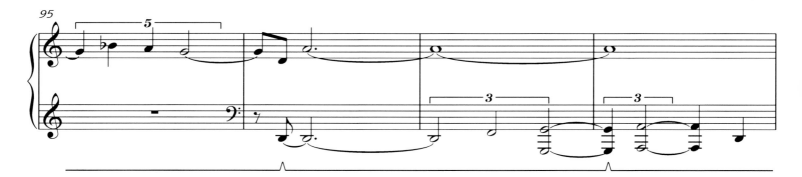

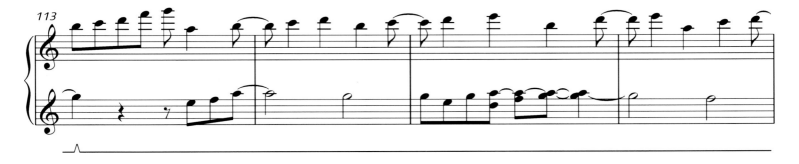

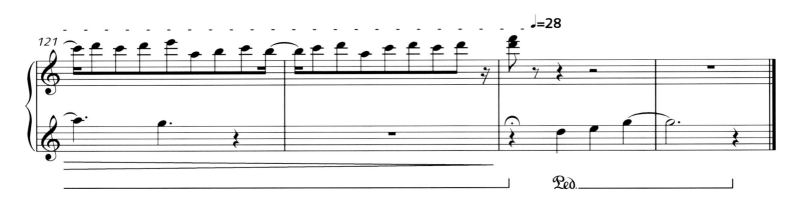